Original title:
Bound by Light

Author: Olivia Oja
ISBN HARDBACK: 978-1-80560-009-1
ISBN PAPERBACK: 978-1-80560-474-7

Light-Laced Memories

In twilight glow, whispers rise,
Soft, tender threads of the skies.
They dance through the years, a gentle breeze,
Woven in dreams, they always please.

Flickers of laughter, echoes of grace,
Moments held fast in a warm embrace.
Time's fleeting touch, like shadows cast,
Carved in the heart, forever to last.

When daylight fades, and stars ignite,
The past glimmers bright, a stunning sight.
Each memory shines with a radiant hue,
Light-laced reflections, both old and new.

In the quiet stillness, memories flow,
Past paths of joy where the soft winds blow.
A tapestry rich with warmth and light,
Guiding the soul through the depths of night.

So let us cherish these moments shared,
In the heart's gallery, forever prepared.
For though we may wander, drift, and roam,
These light-laced memories lead us home.

Forever Illuminated

In the warmth of the night,
Dreams take their flight,
Whispers of hope rise,
Beneath the moon's eyes.

Stars twinkle above,
A blanket of love,
Guiding our way,
In the soft light's sway.

Moments we cherish,
Never to perish,
Carried in hearts,
As each day departs.

Through shadows we wander,
With hearts that ponder,
Endless horizons call,
In the night's sprawl.

Forever we shine bright,
In the endless night,
Together we'll roam,
In this cosmic home.

Starlit Promises

Promises woven in light,
Dancing stars take flight,
Glimmers of trust shine,
In the dark, they combine.

With every heartbeat near,
Whispers of dreams clear,
Under the vast sky,
We vow not to shy.

Fates intertwined tight,
Guiding through the night,
Hand in hand we stand,
On this starlit land.

Echoes of laughter ring,
As the nightbirds sing,
Magic surrounds us,
In the love we trust.

Together we will rise,
Reaching for the skies,
Starlit promises made,
In the glow, we wade.

Light's Gentle Caress

The dawn's first embrace,
Whispers on my face,
Glimmers of new day,
Chasing night away.

With each tender beam,
Life begins to gleam,
Colors brush the morn,
In beauty reborn.

Light dances on leaves,
A symphony weaves,
Nature's sweet refrain,
Washing away pain.

Soft shadows disperse,
In the light's sweet purse,
Hope sings in the air,
A promise, we share.

Finding joy in grace,
In this sacred space,
Light's gentle caress,
Brings forth our happiness.

A Journey in Glow

Set forth on this quest,
With hearts full of zest,
Through valleys and peaks,
Our spirit it speaks.

Every step we take,
Wonders we awake,
In pathways aglow,
With all that we know.

Shining stars guide us,
Through whispers and fuss,
Knowing we are free,
To be who we'll be.

With laughter and light,
Chasing shadows from sight,
Together we roam,
In this journey home.

A tale yet untold,
In the warmth, we hold,
A journey in glow,
Where love seeks to grow.

Embraced by Dawn

Gentle light breaks through the haze,
Birds awaken, sing their praise.
Morning whispers, soft and clear,
A brand new day, the dawn is here.

Golden rays dance on the dew,
Painting skies in shades so blue.
Nature stirs, life starts anew,
In this moment, hearts break through.

Shadows fade, the night retreats,
Sunrise brings our warmest treats.
Hope emerges with every glow,
In the light, together, we grow.

With each breath, a promise made,
In the light, all fears will fade.
Embraced by dawn, we stand as one,
Together bright, we face the sun.

So let this morning fill our souls,
As life's gentle rhythm takes control.
In every moment, joy awaits,
Embraced by dawn, love never hesitates.

Tides of Brilliance

Waves crash softly on the shore,
Whispers secrets, wanting more.
Moonlit paths on water's face,
Tides of brilliance, a sweet embrace.

Stars reflect on ocean's might,
Guiding sailors through the night.
In the rhythm, hearts align,
Tides of brilliance, so divine.

Every ebb, every flow,
Nature's dance, a graceful show.
With the currents, we are drawn,
To the magic of each dawn.

Shells and treasures in the sand,
Stories told by nature's hand.
Listen closely, hear the song,
Tides of brilliance, we belong.

Together we ride every wave,
In the depths, our spirits brave.
For in each tide, our dreams ignite,
Tides of brilliance, pure delight.

Shimmering Connections

Hands meet softly, hearts entwined,
In the silence, souls aligned.
Glimmers bright, a sacred spark,
Shimmering connections, lighting dark.

Eyes that hold a thousand dreams,
Whispers shared in gentle streams.
In this bond, we find our way,
Shimmering connections, come what may.

Each laugh shared, a golden thread,
Woven stories, softly spread.
Together, we create our space,
Shimmering connections, love's embrace.

Through trials faced and joys combined,
Kindred spirits, hands consigned.
In the dance of life, we twine,
Shimmering connections, pure divine.

So let us cherish every glance,
In this journey, join the dance.
For in connection, we are free,
Shimmering connections, you and me.

Silhouettes of Serenity

Shadowed figures in the glow,
Calm and peace in every flow.
Beneath the stars, we find our place,
Silhouettes of serenity, a gentle grace.

Evening whispers, soft and low,
Guiding hearts wherever they go.
In quiet moments, fears subside,
Silhouettes of serenity, right by our side.

Trees stand tall, against the night,
Holding secrets in their height.
With each rustle, nature sighs,
Silhouettes of serenity, under starlit skies.

Moments linger, time stands still,
In stillness, find your heart's will.
Together, we find harmony,
Silhouettes of serenity, wild and free.

So let us breathe in every hue,
In twilight's embrace, me and you.
For in the silence, beauty reigns,
Silhouettes of serenity, love remains.

A Symphony of Light

In the dawn, soft rays appear,
Whispers of warmth, a gentle cheer.
Colors dance on morning's face,
Nature sings in a warm embrace.

Glowing streams through trees unite,
Casting shadows, chasing night.
Melodies of the heart ignite,
Creating magic, pure and bright.

As the sun begins to rise,
Painting heaven with golden dyes.
A canvas vast, it draws the view,
Each moment feels forever new.

In the twilight, colors blend,
A symphony that will not end.
The stars will come and light the skies,
A lullaby, where spirit flies.

With each beat, time stands still,
A radiant pulse, a shared thrill.
Together in this vibrant space,
The world unfolds a warm embrace.

Luminous Pathways

Footsteps traced on vibrant ground,
Whispers of dreams in the surround.
Guided by a soft, warm glow,
Every path a tale to show.

Through the forest, light calls clear,
Illuminating all that's dear.
Leaves aglow with stories told,
In soft hues of orange and gold.

As we wander, feelings blend,
Silent moments, hearts extend.
Every shadow holds a trace,
Of laughter shared, a warm embrace.

With each turn, new sights delight,
Nature's song, a pure delight.
Walk with me, where dreams ignite,
Together in this shimm'ring light.

Radiant Threads

Stitched with care, dreams intertwine,
With every step, your hand in mine.
Golden threads in fabric spun,
Together weaving, we are one.

Across horizons, the colors blend,
Strength and beauty, our hearts mend.
In the tapestry of the night,
Radiance flows, a guiding light.

Through valleys deep and mountains high,
Weaving stories, you and I.
Each thread glimmers, pure and bright,
A history rich, a shared delight.

In this quilt, love is the seam,
Holding tight to every dream.
With silver rays, in shadows dance,
Together, we take every chance.

Every woven twist, every turn,
In our hearts, a fire burns.
As long as life continues to flow,
Radiant threads of love will grow.

Together in Brilliance

Underneath the starlit sky,
We transform as moments fly.
Side by side, we find our place,
In this world, a warm embrace.

The moonlit path calls us near,
Every heartbeat loud and clear.
With every whisper, fears take flight,
Together, we embrace the night.

Through the shadows, our spirits dance,
In this rhythm, we take a chance.
Each radiant spark ignites our dreams,
Connecting us with vibrant beams.

In the silence, love speaks loud,
Among the stars, we stand so proud.
As brilliant souls, we intertwine,
Together, our light will always shine.

Hand in hand, we journey far,
Guided by each twinkling star.
In unity, our spirits soar,
Together, we are evermore.

Woven in Brightness

Threads of gold in the sky,
Weaving tales of the sun,
Whispers of warmth and light,
Creating dreams, one by one.

Colors dance on the breeze,
Brushing hearts with their grace,
In the fabric of the world,
We find our true embrace.

Each sunrise tells a story,
Of hopes that gently rise,
Shadows fade in glory,
As laughter paints the skies.

In the hues of twilight,
We gather memories bright,
A tapestry of moments,
That shimmer in the night.

Embracing every shade,
In this woven delight,
We dance through endless journeys,
Woven in brightness, bright.

Resilience in Radiance

Through the storm and through the rain,
Hearts emerge, unbroken, bold,
In the face of fleeting pain,
We find the strength to hold.

Like flowers after the frost,
We rise with vibrant grace,
In the warmth, no love is lost,
Resilience finds its place.

Each challenge that we face,
Turns to a spark of light,
In shadows, we embrace,
A journey filled with might.

When the night seems too long,
Hope's whisper calls us near,
In the silence, we belong,
Radiance conquers fear.

With every step we take,
New paths begin to bloom,
In our hearts, a bright ache,
Resilience lights the room.

Harmony of Light

In the dawn's embracing glow,
Nature sings a soothing tune,
Ripples in a quiet flow,
Beneath the watchful moon.

Stars above in perfect dance,
Twinkling like forgotten dreams,
In this cosmic happenstance,
Life's magic softly gleams.

Every heartbeats in sync,
With the pulse of earth and sky,
In the spaces where we think,
Harmonies will never die.

From the mountains to the sea,
Every moment feels just right,
Together, you and me,
Living in this harmony of light.

With each breath, a gentle sigh,
As we find our way back home,
In the colors that we dye,
Harmony in light has grown.

Celestial Ties

Underneath the starry dome,
We search for our place above,
In the universe, our home,
Wrapped in cosmic threads of love.

Galaxies spin in a dance,
Mysterious, vast, and wide,
In this endless cosmic chance,
We find our souls collide.

With each breath of the night,
And every glimmering star,
We remember our shared light,
And how close we really are.

Whispers swirl through the skies,
As comets blaze on their quest,
In their tails, our dreams arise,
Celestial ties manifest.

Through the darkness, we will shine,
Bound by love's strong embrace,
In this dance, you are mine,
Celestial ties, our grace.

Yearning for the Shine

In the twilight, shadows grow,
A whisper calls from deep below.
Stars twinkle with a gentle sigh,
Awakening dreams that dare to fly.

Hope blooms like the morning light,
Chasing away the dim of night.
With every breath, the heart does yearn,
For the spark of love's sweet return.

Lost in a maze of fading stars,
The path winds on, marred by scars.
Yet through the dark, a flame ignites,
Guiding hearts on starry nights.

Together we chase horizons wide,
Hand in hand, with love as our guide.
Yearning for spark, for warmth, for shine,
In the depths of night, your hand in mine.

Let the moonlight dance on dreams,
Illuminating all that gleams.
With every moment, we will find,
A world of wonders, intertwined.

Latticework of Glistening Dreams

Threads of silver weave the night,
Glistening stars, a wondrous sight.
In the fabric, hearts entwine,
Crafting tales that feel divine.

Each dream a pattern, spun with care,
Latticework of hopes laid bare.
We reach for wishes, bright and bold,
In the story that's yet to be told.

Whispers echo in the air,
Calling souls to those who dare.
With every stitch, a memory shared,
In the tapestry, our hearts declared.

Moments captured, sewn in time,
In unison, our hearts will chime.
Glistening dreams coat the night,
Guided onward by love's pure light.

Together we'll mend what once was torn,
A lattice rich, since hope was born.
In every seam, our spirits gleam,
A dance of fate, a shared dream.

Celestial Bondage

Underneath the velvet skies,
Celestial bonds, where silence lies.
Stars are anchored in fate's design,
Binding hearts, both yours and mine.

In the cosmos, whispers flow,
Telling tales only we know.
Captured souls in a timeless spree,
Forever bound, you and me.

Galaxies spin with radiant grace,
Our love's embrace, a sacred space.
Lightyears stretch, yet we remain,
In this dance, both joy and pain.

As comets streak across the night,
Our spirits soar, a shared flight.
In cosmic arms, we find our place,
Celestial bondage, an endless grace.

Together we explore the skies,
In the starlight where spirit flies.
In every star and moonlit glow,
Our bond shines bright, forever aglow.

Echoes of the Sun's Caress

Morning whispers, soft and warm,
Echoes dance, a sweet alarm.
Sunlight spills across the land,
Nature's gift, a gentle hand.

Golden rays embrace the trees,
Swaying softly in the breeze.
Each bloom drinks the light with glee,
A tapestry of tender harmony.

Close your eyes, let shadows flee,
Feel the sun's warm symphony.
In its glow, a world reborn,
As night retreats and breaks the dawn.

Footsteps follow the path of light,
Guided by the sun so bright.
Echoes linger in the air,
In the warmth of love laid bare.

Let the sunlight kiss your face,
With each touch, a soft embrace.
Echoes of a day so blessed,
In the sun's caress, we find our rest.

Illuminated Journeys

On paths of light, we wander far,
With dreams aglow like evening stars.
Each step we take, a tale unfolds,
In whispered shadows, secrets told.

Through valleys deep, and mountains high,
The lanterns guide where hopes can fly.
In twilight's hue, our hearts align,
With every spark, a new design.

The road ahead is steep and bright,
With every challenge, we find our light.
Those moments shared, sweet, profound,
In every laugh, true joy is found.

Together we chase the morning sun,
Hand in hand, we'll always run.
The journey rich with love's embrace,
Every heartbeat, a sacred space.

In dreams we forge our destiny,
As pathways merge in harmony.
These illuminated journeys weave,
The fabric of what we believe.

The Glow Between Us

In silence shared, our spirits dance,
A subtle spark, a fleeting glance.
With whispered words, our souls ignite,
Beneath the stars, we find our light.

Through every storm, our hearts will glow,
A guiding fire in the undertow.
With every beat, a rhythm flows,
In this embrace, our love still grows.

Each moment cherished, bright and dear,
As shadows fade, we draw near.
In the warmth of trust, we intertwine,
The glow between us, pure and divine.

Through the darkest nights, we fiercely shine,
Creating warmth, our hearts align.
In every silence, in every sound,
A glow unites where love is found.

Together we forge a light that's true,
A brilliance shared, just me and you.
In this sacred space, we find our way,
The glow between us will never sway.

Luminous Bonds

In laughter shared, our spirits rise,
With every hug, a spark replies.
A bond that's woven, deep and bright,
In every glance, true love's delight.

With threads of gold, our story's spun,
In every day, two hearts are one.
Through trials faced, we find the way,
These luminous bonds will always stay.

Through whispered dreams and tender sighs,
The glow we share will never die.
In every memory, warmth ignites,
These luminous bonds are pure delights.

As seasons change, we're ever near,
The warmth of love will persevere.
In every shadow, we find the light,
Together we stand, hearts shining bright.

With every step into the unknown,
These luminous bonds, forever grown.
In life's grand dance, we'll always find,
Love's gentle glow, so intertwined.

A Symphony of Sparks

In the quiet night, a spark ignites,
Creating music, pure delights.
With every note, our hearts will sing,
A symphony of sparks in spring.

With rhythmic beats, we move as one,
In every laugh, the joy begun.
A dance of light, a vivid trance,
In every glance, a bold romance.

Through every challenge, we stay in tune,
With echoes sweet beneath the moon.
Our laughter swells, a vibrant score,
Creating warmth, we long for more.

Together we write this song of dreams,
In harmony, our spirit beams.
With notes of love, we'll soar so high,
In this symphony that will never die.

As stars align and shadows fade,
In every spark, our love cascades.
This symphony will echo far,
Through every heart, we shine like stars.

Celestial Cords

In the night sky, stars align,
Whispers of fate intertwine.
Silken strands of cosmic thread,
Binding souls where dreams are fed.

Galaxies dance in endless grace,
Time and space, a warm embrace.
Each heartbeat echoes in the void,
In bonds of love, we are enjoyed.

Celestial tides, we float and flow,
Guided by light, we come to know.
Through the shadows, we will steer,
Together in the atmosphere.

Beneath the veil, a secret shared,
Invisible ties, forever paired.
Unity forged through the night,
In harmony, we find our light.

As the dawn breaks, colors blend,
Echoes of promises suspend.
Cords that stretch beyond the sphere,
In the universe, we persevere.

A Fabric of Kindred Light

Threads of gold weave through the dark,
Creating patterns, a vibrant spark.
Each moment stitched with care and grace,
We find solace in this place.

A tapestry of shared delight,
Every glimpse a guiding light.
In this fabric, hearts unite,
A warmth that banishes the night.

Colors blend with each new day,
Kindred spirits find their way.
In every seam, a story waits,
Binding fates through open gates.

Woven dreams take flight and soar,
Each heartbeat echoes evermore.
In the loom of life, we stand strong,
Together, where we all belong.

As the sunset paints the sky,
In each strand, a sweet goodbye.
Yet in our hearts, the threads remain,
A fabric of joy, woven in pain.

Threads of the Infinite

In the void, threads stretch unseen,
Tales of old, whispers keen.
Infinite paths, we walk with care,
Connecting dreams laid bare.

Each thread a story, rich and bold,
Ancient wisdom, flowers unfold.
Weaving moments as they flow,
In this dance, we come to know.

The cosmos hums a tune divine,
In every echo, hearts align.
Threads of fate, entwined we stand,
Together, hand in hand.

Through the fabric of time we roam,
Guided by light, we find our home.
Each twist and turn, a lesson learned,
In the fire, our spirits burned.

As we journey through the night,
Threads illuminate the plight.
Boundless dreams, forever we trace,
In the infinite, we find our place.

Emblems of the Dawn

At the break of day, the world awakes,
Emblems rise, the silence breaks.
A canvas painted, new and bright,
Hope emerges with the light.

Birds take wing in morning's glow,
Songs of joy begin to flow.
With every ray, a promise made,
In the dawn, fears start to fade.

The sun bestows its gentle grace,
Awakening hearts in every place.
Together, we embrace the morn,
In unity, we are reborn.

As shadows melt, we chase our dreams,
Life unfolds in vibrant beams.
Emblems of love, we hold them tight,
In every moment, pure delight.

Whispers carry on the breeze,
Reminders of what brings us peace.
In the dawn's embrace, we rise anew,
Bound by hope, our spirits true.

Merging of Souls

In the quiet of the night,
Two spirits intertwine,
Whispers of a secret light,
Boundless love, divine.

In the dance of shadows cast,
Hearts beat in perfect time,
Moments lost, forever vast,
Harmony in every rhyme.

Through the storms, they find their way,
Guided by a gentle grace,
Even when the skies turn gray,
Together, they embrace.

Each gaze a whispered vow,
In silence, they ignite,
This bond, they will allow,
To shine both day and night.

Two souls as one, they soar,
Where love knows no bounds,
In the ocean's endless roar,
Eternal peace surrounds.

Radiance of Togetherness

Underneath the silver moon,
Hands clasped, hearts aligned,
In this moment, love attunes,
Unity intertwined.

Soft laughter fills the air,
A melody so sweet,
In every glance, they share,
Their journey feels complete.

Side by side, they face the dawn,
With dreams that intertwine,
Each moment brings a bond,
A treasure, truly fine.

Through shadows and the light,
They weave a vibrant tale,
With every gentle fight,
Love's colors never pale.

In the warmth of their embrace,
Lifetime whispers flow,
With every breath, a trace,
Of love's unending glow.

Flickering Hearts

In twilight's softest glow,
Two hearts begin to dance,
With every ebb and flow,
Life offers them a chance.

Glimmers spark in the night,
Promises softly spoken,
With every shared delight,
Love's fragile bonds unbroken.

Winds carry whispered dreams,
As starlight paints the sky,
In moments, hope redeems,
Together, they will fly.

Every flicker tells a story,
Of paths they dared to choose,
In the glow of love's glory,
No fear is left to lose.

Hearts intertwined, aglow,
In shadows, they will beam,
With every blush and flow,
They live their endless dream.

Illuminated Paths

Beneath the arching trees,
Footsteps softly blend,
With every breath, a breeze,
They walk, hearts free to mend.

Through gardens filled with light,
They share each joyous tale,
As day slips into night,
Their love, a glowing trail.

With every turn they take,
New wonders come to view,
In each choice that they make,
Their spirits feel anew.

The moonlight guides them on,
As stars begin to gleam,
In every stubborn dawn,
Together, they will dream.

United in their quest,
Through paths both dark and bright,
In the journey, they are blessed,
Illuminated light.

Beyond the Horizon's Glow

The sun dips low, a fiery hue,
Whispers of night in twilight's view.
Stars awaken in the fading light,
Dreams take flight on the canvas of night.

Waves of silver kiss the shore,
The ocean hums in a cosmic roar.
Beyond the reach, where visions soar,
Hope ignites on the distant moor.

Clouds embrace the fading blaze,
Casting shadows in a jeweled haze.
Each heartbeat echoes in the dark,
A gentle sigh, a shimmering spark.

The world transforms in hues divine,
Silhouettes dance on the edge of time.
In the stillness, magic flows,
Beyond the horizon's infinite glow.

Tethered to the Radiance

In the hush of dawn's sweet grace,
Light unfurls with a soft embrace.
A tether formed of golden beams,
Binding souls to their wildest dreams.

Fields of daisies in bloom arise,
Painting the earth with laughter and sighs.
Under the arc of the azure dome,
Hearts unite in their cosmic home.

Through valleys deep, we roam and play,
With whispers of light guiding our way.
Every moment, a sparkling chance,
As we sway in the universe's dance.

Stars align in a sacred thread,
Carving paths where hope is spread.
Together we soar, unbound and free,
Tethered to the radiance, just you and me.

Dances of Ethereal Fire

In the midst of night, whispers ignite,
Celestial flames flicker, taking flight.
A ballet of light on the velvet sky,
As galaxies twirl, they giggle and sigh.

Comets dash with a streaking flair,
While constellations weave tales in the air.
Each twinkle a note in the cosmic song,
Inviting the lost to join where they belong.

Echoes of laughter ripple through space,
Velvet shadows in a shimmering lace.
With every pulse, the universe spins,
In dances of fire, where wonder begins.

Awakened dreams in the starry choir,
Lost in the rhythm of ethereal fire.
A spectacle bright that stirs the soul,
An endless embrace, a cosmic scroll.

Constellations of the Heart

In the silence deep, a whisper calls,
Mapping the journey as the stardust falls.
Each heart a constellation, bright and bold,
Stories of love in the night unfold.

Through layers of time, we dance and weave,
In the shadows, we choose to believe.
Fleeting moments like meteor trails,
Guide us home where the heart prevails.

Silver threads bind the vast unknown,
In the tapestry of love, we've grown.
Each pulse a promise, a tethered song,
In constellations, we both belong.

As we wander beneath the starry sky,
In the heart's embrace, we will never say goodbye.
Exploring the depths, twin flames ignite,
In the constellations of love's pure light.

Twinkling Together

Under skies so vast and deep,
Stars come out, their secrets to keep.
Winking softly, they share their light,
Guiding dreams through the silent night.

In the stillness, hearts align,
With whispers soft, like aged wine.
Moments linger, time stands still,
Together we dance, our spirits thrill.

Waves of laughter, a cosmic thread,
Stories written, words unsaid.
Hand in hand, we trace the glow,
The magic of love, forever flow.

Beneath the moon, we make a vow,
To cherish each twinkle, here and now.
In unity, we find our song,
Twinkling together, where we belong.

So let us shine, both near and far,
In the night sky, we are the stars.
With every heartbeat, a promise made,
In the dance of light, never to fade.

Spectrum of Belonging

In colors bright, we find our place,
A canvas rich, a warm embrace.
Different hues, yet intertwined,
In diversity, our strength we find.

The reds and blues, the greens and golds,
Every story of love unfolds.
We gather round, a vibrant scene,
In each other's arms, we are seen.

Echoes of laughter fill the air,
Sharing moments beyond compare.
A tapestry woven with threads so fine,
In the spectrum of love, we all shine.

With open hearts, we face the dawn,
Together we rise, forever drawn.
Through trials faced, we stand as one,
In the dance of life, the race is run.

So here we stand, a chorus strong,
In the spectrum of belonging, we belong.
United in dreams, we'll rise anew,
For in this world, I find you true.

Unraveled by Dawn

Night recedes, a gentle sigh,
Whispers of dreams, as stars say goodbye.
The golden light begins to creep,
Stirring the world from its tender sleep.

Shadows shrink, as warmth unfolds,
Cloaks of darkness, now retreating bold.
Kisses of sunlight, soft and sweet,
Awakening life beneath our feet.

Birds take flight, their songs like fire,
Binding our hearts with raw desire.
With every moment, the past unspools,
Under dawn's gaze, we are the fools.

Yet in the glow, there's hope renewed,
In the light, our fears subdued.
Unraveled threads weave stories clear,
With every sunrise, we persevere.

So let the dawn embrace the day,
In its warmth, we've found our way.
In the dance of light, we find our grace,
Unraveled by dawn, we embrace.

Reflections of the Soul

In quiet waters, the truth we seek,
Mirrored depths where hearts can speak.
Every ripple tells a tale,
Of dreams and hopes that never pale.

Glimmers of light on the surface shine,
Illuminating the paths divine.
In solitude, we find our voice,
With every glance, we make a choice.

The depths within, a sacred space,
A journey inward, a gentle race.
Peeling layers, we uncover gold,
Reflections of stories waiting to be told.

So let us dive and venture deep,
Into the stillness, our secrets keep.
In the soul's mirror, we come alive,
In this quiet dance, we learn to thrive.

With every glance, the truth unfolds,
In reflections of the soul, we behold.
Together we wander, hand in hand,
In the depths of self, we understand.

A Dance with the Divine

In the stillness of the night,
Stars whisper secrets, pure and bright.
I reach for dreams that soar and glide,
In the embrace of the divine.

Moonlit shadows softly sway,
Guiding thoughts that drift away.
Every heartbeat sings a tune,
A dance beneath the silver moon.

The breeze carries tales of old,
Stories of love, daring and bold.
In this moment, time stands still,
I yield my heart to fate's kind will.

The cosmos glimmers, vast and wide,
In this journey, I abide.
Each twirl a testament of grace,
In the grasp of the divine space.

With every step, I find my way,
In the light of dawn's first ray.
Together, we shall intertwine,
In a dance that feels divine.

Radiant Echoes

Softly spoken, words like light,
Illuminate the endless night.
Every echo, rich and clear,
Whispers dreams that draw us near.

In the garden, blooms alive,
Each petal holds a sacred vibe.
Nature's voice, a symphony,
In radiant echoes, we are free.

Time flows gently, like a stream,
Moments captured, love's sweet dream.
In the warmth of shared delight,
Hearts converge in purest sight.

Through valleys deep, and mountains high,
We chase the sun across the sky.
Together, we shall carve our fate,
In radiant echoes, love awaits.

Let the world fade, peace unfold,
In a tapestry of gold.
In every heartbeat, every sigh,
Radiant echoes never die.

Luminous Connections

Beneath the sky's expansive hue,
Hearts collide where dreams come true.
In silent moments, souls align,
Creating bonds, so pure, divine.

Every glance, a spark ignites,
In the dark, we find our lights.
Together, we weave bright threads,
Of laughter, love, and whispered reds.

The universe conspires close,
With every breath, we feel what's most.
In the dance of fate, we find,
Luminous connections, intertwined.

As twilight whispers sweet goodbyes,
Our spirits soar, we touch the skies.
In unity, we rise and fall,
Luminous connections, binding us all.

Time may shift, seasons may change,
Yet this bond, it will not estrange.
Forever etched, a sacred sign,
In luminous connections, we align.

Chasing Sunbeams

Across the hills, the sun does rise,
Painting gold in morning skies.
With each ray, hope takes its flight,
Chasing sunbeams, pure delight.

In fields of green, the flowers sway,
Embracing warmth of the new day.
With laughter bright, we run and play,
In this dance, come what may.

Every shimmer, every glow,
Guides us forth where dreams will flow.
With joyous hearts, we shall explore,
Chasing sunbeams forevermore.

As shadows stretch and daylight wanes,
We gather love, like summer rains.
In twilight's hue, our spirits gleam,
Chasing sunbeams, living the dream.

Though dusk may bring its gentle sigh,
We'll hold the warmth, let spirits fly.
In every heart, let love redeem,
Chasing sunbeams, our timeless theme.

Whispers of the Celestial

In the hush of night, stars gleam bright,
Softly whispering tales of light.
Moonlit shadows dance on trees,
Carried on a gentle breeze.

Dreamers gaze up, spirits soar,
Chasing remnants, wanting more.
Time stands still in cosmic grace,
Embracing each celestial face.

Hearts alight with hopes unbound,
In the silence, magic found.
Galaxies spin in endless song,
Where the soul feels it belongs.

Through the dark, a spark can grow,
Painting skies with love's warm glow.
Every twinkle bears a name,
In the universe, none are the same.

So listen close, let your heart feel,
The whispers of the stars reveal.
In every night, a tale is spun,
With celestial love, we're all as one.

Luminary Echoes

Light years away, echoes call,
Fainting voices that gently fall.
Guided by the stars' soft sight,
In the silence, shines the light.

Hearts resonate under bright skies,
Where dreams linger and hope never dies.
In the glow, wanderers find,
Connections forever entwined.

Each flicker, each glimmer, a chance,
To sway with the universe's dance.
In the vastness, love unites,
Bringing warmth through chilly nights.

Reflections of paths we once roamed,
In the stellar vastness, we feel at home.
Every luminosity spins a tale,
On vibrant winds, our spirits sail.

So let the echoes guide your way,
To the places where we wish to stay.
For in the light, we all can see,
The luminary heart of you and me.

Spheres of Glistening Dreams

In a realm where wishes gleam,
Lives the essence of a dream.
Floating softly on silver streams,
Wrapped in halos of moonbeams.

Every joy a starry sphere,
Reflecting hopes that draw us near.
In the tapestry night-laced skies,
Galaxies where the spirit flies.

Through the veil of tender night,
Hidden realms, a surreal sight.
In the hush, possibilities bloom,
Painting life in vibrant hues.

Dreamers cast their hearts so wide,
Journeying forth with faith as guide.
In each sphere that glistens bright,
Whispers cradle lost delight.

With every dream, a story spun,
In the universe, we are all one.
So chase the glimmers, let them beam,
Live within the glistening dream.

The Ties That Illuminate

Across the distance, hearts align,
Woven threads in perfect design.
In gentle whispers, bonds take flight,
With every heartbeat, shining bright.

Little moments, fragile and small,
Create a tapestry that binds us all.
In shadows cast, our spirits dance,
Chasing dreams, embracing chance.

Through the storms, we hold on tight,
Finding solace in shared light.
In the chaos, love remains,
Navigating through joy and pains.

Echoed laughter, unfurling grace,
Each soft glance, a warm embrace.
In timeless space, our souls will glow,
Illuminating paths we know.

So let the ties that bind us gleam,
Fulfilling every cherished dream.
In this journey, hand in hand,
Together, we will ever stand.

Enchanted by Glow

In the hush of twilight's grace,
Whispers dance in the space.
Stars flicker, dreams align,
Hearts soar where hopes entwine.

Moonlight casts its gentle beam,
Guiding souls in a dream.
Nature's breath, a soft embrace,
Every moment held in place.

Through the trees, the fireflies gleam,
Illuminating the midnight theme.
The world wrapped in silver's thread,
Each shadow secrets spread.

Life unfolds with magic's art,
Every glow a beating heart.
In the stillness, magic flows,
Time pauses where love grows.

Lost in wonder, we explore,
Hand in hand, forevermore.
In this enchanted dance we find,
A glow that binds us, spirit entwined.

Under the Glistening Skies

Beneath the wide and cherished dome,
Wanderers find their true home.
Where clouds brush the mountains high,
And dreams stretch to the open sky.

Stars spill secrets from above,
Whispering tales of hope and love.
The universe in quiet cries,
All we seek under glistening skies.

The evening breeze, a gentle tune,
Carried forth by a silver moon.
Every breath a chance to soar,
With every heartbeat, we explore.

Night reveals a canvas bright,
Painting shadows with soft light.
In this realm where wishes rise,
Life unfolds 'neath glistening skies.

Hand in hand, we'll face the dawn,
As night gives way to a new song.
Embraced by dreams that never die,
Together, we thrive and fly.

Stories Written in Light

In the glow of morning's kiss,
Every moment feels like bliss.
Sunbeams dance on petals wide,
Nature's truths we cannot hide.

Golden rays paint the day,
Illuminating every way.
In shadows, stories softly bloom,
Whispers of life in every room.

Through the night, the stars will tell,
Tales of joy and tales of bell.
Each flicker bears a tale so bright,
Stories woven in pure light.

The flicker of a candle's flame,
Echoes of love, never the same.
In every heartbeat, a million sights,
Life's sweetest stories, boundless heights.

In the fabric of our living,
Every shadow, a call for giving.
Together, let our journeys ignite,
As we write our stories in light.

Embraced by Shimmer

In a world where dreams take flight,
We chase the spark of endless light.
Every moment holds a gem,
Whispers of joy, a cherished hymn.

Dancing shadows, soft and clear,
Echoes of laughter, we hold dear.
In the shimmer, magic sways,
Guiding us through vibrant days.

The gentle breeze upon our skin,
Wraps us in love, a soft din.
Together, we rise, forever bold,
In this embrace, our stories told.

With every heartbeat, we ignite,
A glow that conquers endless night.
In shimmering paths, we wander free,
Boundless souls, you and me.

Through life's dance, we find the song,
In each other, where we belong.
Embraced by shimmer, hand in hand,
Together, forever we stand.

Harmony in Brilliance

In the dawn's soft touch, light grows,
Birds in symphony, the world knows.
Leaves dance gently with the breeze,
Nature's song brings hearts to ease.

Shadows stretch as day unfolds,
Whispers of secrets yet untold.
Colors merge in vibrant skies,
Painting dreams where hope can rise.

In moments shared, we find our tune,
Underneath the watchful moon.
Together we weave a radiant thread,
In the tapestry of life, we're led.

With laughter bright, we overcome,
Hand in hand, we become one.
Every heartbeat, every glance,
In perfect rhythm, we find our dance.

A symphony of hearts entwined,
In harmony, our souls aligned.
Through every trial, every cheer,
In brilliance bask, we persevere.

The Call of the Shimmering

In twilight's glow, the stars appear,
Their shimmering light beckons near.
Whispers of hope fill the night,
Illuminating paths of delight.

Softly they twinkle, secrets to share,
A celestial dance, beyond compare.
Inviting souls to dream and soar,
With every flicker, they implore.

As the moon drapes her silver veil,
Echoes of magic begin to sail.
Heartbeats sync with heavenly calls,
In the silence, love never stalls.

Each glimmer holds a story bright,
Woven threads of dreams in flight.
Guiding hearts through shadowed fears,
In the shimmering, joy appears.

With every glance, we feel their pull,
Craving the light, a heart so full.
Together we chase the starlit streams,
In the call of the shimmering, we find our dreams.

Trails of Glowing Moments

In the quiet hours of the night,
Stars twinkle with gentle light.
Each moment glows with gentle grace,
Time slows down, a warm embrace.

Footsteps lead through paths of gold,
Every memory, a tale retold.
Whispers linger, soft and sweet,
In glowing moments, we feel complete.

The laughter shared, the smiles bright,
Moments that sparkle, pure delight.
In every hug and every sigh,
Memories linger, they never die.

As dawn arrives, we hold them near,
Each sparkling trace, a reason to cheer.
With gratitude for what we've shared,
In trails of glowing, we're truly bared.

In life's grand journey, we find our light,
Through trails of glowing, hearts take flight.
Together we'll create a spark,
In this tapestry, we leave our mark.

Starlit Affinity

Under starlit skies so deep,
Silent promises we keep.
In the night's embrace, we dance,
Our hearts ignited, pure romance.

Constellations weave our tale,
In the dark, love will prevail.
Every glance, a spark divine,
In this cosmos, you are mine.

Whispers travel on the air,
In your gaze, I find my prayer.
Together we dream, together we fly,
Anchored in love as time goes by.

The universe sings our song,
In this bond, we both belong.
With every heartbeat, our spirits soar,
In starlit affinity, forevermore.

As the planets align above,
In every moment, I feel your love.
Hand in hand through the night we roam,
In the starlit skies, we find our home.

Twinkles of Eternity

Stars above, they gleam so bright,
In the silence of the night.
Whispers of dreams softly soar,
In the space forevermore.

Time stands still, a pause in grace,
Memories dance, they find their place.
Moments captured, hearts entwined,
In the tapestry of the mind.

Hope is cradled in each flash,
Echoing in a fleeting dash.
A glint, a spark, a timeless sign,
In the universe, we align.

Fates interwoven, threads of gold,
Stories shared, yet to be told.
In the dark, we find our way,
Guided by the light of day.

Twinkles fade but never die,
Reborn beneath a velvet sky.
A dance through ages, ever free,
In twinkles of eternity.

Veins of Twilight

When the sun dips low and sighs,
Golden hues paint the skies.
Shadows stretch, the world at rest,
In twilight's arms, we feel blessed.

Velvet whispers in the air,
Embracing tales, with love to share.
Every heartbeat, soft and slow,
Where dreamers roam and spirits glow.

Darkness beckons with its charm,
Holding us in a gentle calm.
Between the day and night we find,
Veins of twilight, hearts aligned.

Moonlight dances, casting spells,
In the silence, magic swells.
Canvas painted with each breath,
Life unfolds, defying death.

In this hour, we deeply feel,
The woven dreams, the unreal.
Through the dusk, we see the way,
In the twilight, we shall stay.

Whispering Candles

Flickering light in the stillness,
Softly speaks of the fullness.
Each flame a story, gently spun,
Whispers echo, one by one.

In the dark, a guiding star,
Illuminating from afar.
Memories flicker, shadows cast,
In the moments, forever last.

Gathered close, we share the glow,
Hearts entwined as embers flow.
With every breath, peace takes flight,
Wrapped in warmth, lost in light.

Candlelight dances on the wall,
Filling spaces, embracing all.
In its warmth, our hopes convene,
In whispering candles, love is seen.

As they burn, our spirits rise,
Reflecting dreams that touch the skies.
In the quiet, strength ignites,
Through whispering candles, we find sights.

The Glow of Unity

Hands entwined, a sacred bond,
Together we rise, we respond.
In this glow, our hearts ignite,
Shining bright, dispelling night.

Voices harmonize, sweet and clear,
In this moment, we draw near.
One heartbeat blends a symphony,
In the glow of unity.

Branches reaching, roots embrace,
A tapestry, each thread in place.
Together strong, we face the storm,
In love's light, we are reborn.

Every difference, a vibrant hue,
Colors of life in shades so true.
In this glow, we break the chain,
And dance through joy, despite the pain.

Together we shine, forever bright,
Illuminating through the night.
In our hearts, a flame we see,
In the glow of unity, we are free.

Sparks of Togetherness

In the warmth of shared laughter,
Hearts ignite like a flame.
Moments intertwine softly,
Together, never the same.

We dance in the glow of twilight,
Counting stars in the night.
Hand in hand through the shadows,
Our spirits taking flight.

Each whisper, a precious secret,
Binding souls in delight.
With every glance, we discover,
Love blooms, pure and bright.

In the tapestry of memories,
We weave our dreams with care.
Every touch tells a story,
Echoing the love we share.

Through the storms and the sunshine,
Together, we find our way.
In the heart of togetherness,
Forever we choose to stay.

Celestial Embrace

Underneath the starlit canopy,
We find solace, heart to heart.
Whispers of the cosmos call us,
In their love, we play our part.

Galaxies swirl in our visions,
Drawing us to endless nights.
In the silence, we become one,
Lost in the softest lights.

The universe spins around us,
With each pulse, our spirits soar.
In the depths of this connection,
We crave for nothing more.

Through constellations and shadows,
Your laughter sounds like a song.
In this celestial embrace,
Together, we both belong.

As time dances through the heavens,
We cherish every kiss.
Wrapped in this cosmic wonder,
Eternal moments of bliss.

Moonlit Affection

Beneath the gentle moonlight,
Your eyes sparkle with dreams.
In this soft, silvery glow,
Love flows like whispered streams.

We walk on paths of stardust,
Hand in hand, hearts aglow.
Every step speaks of magic,
In the night, we softly flow.

The world fades into silence,
As our shadows intertwine.
In this moonlit affection,
Your heart forever is mine.

With each laugh shared between us,
The moon nods in delight.
In the stillness, our souls dance,
Two stars lost in the night.

So let's cherish these moments,
As the moon watches our play.
In the glow of our connection,
Together, we'll always stay.

The Brightest Silence

In the quiet of the evening,
We find peace in our breath.
No words break this still moment,
Just love that conquers death.

With a gaze that speaks volumes,
Our hearts converse with grace.
In this brightest silence,
We find our sacred space.

Every heartbeat a reminder,
Of the bond we have formed.
In the hush, we grow closer,
A love forever warmed.

Like the stars in the twilight,
Shining bright against the dark.
In this calm, we discover,
Together we leave our mark.

So let the world keep spinning,
As we remain side by side.
In the brightness of this silence,
Our souls will forever confide.

Unseen Currents of Light

In shadows deep, a whisper glows,
A pulse of life that softly flows.
Through hidden paths, our fates entwine,
Ethereal threads, both yours and mine.

With gentlest breeze, it tugs the soul,
A silent call, to make us whole.
We dance along the veiled embrace,
In unseen currents, find our place.

A shimmer here, a flicker there,
A spark ignites the midnight air.
Together, though we may not see,
These currents bind you close to me.

In every heartbeat, every sigh,
An energy we can't deny.
Like stars that flicker in the night,
We shine together, pure delight.

So trust the pull, let shadows sway,
For love's true path will find its way.
In the unseen, magic gleams,
Our bond ignites eternal dreams.

Luminescent Ties

Threads of gold in twilight spun,
A tapestry where hearts are one.
Through every laugh, through every tear,
These ties of light forever near.

With every step, a path unfolds,
In every moment, the warmth holds.
We journey far, we venture wide,
With luminescent love as guide.

In silent nights, under the stars,
We carry light, despite the scars.
A glow that guides us through the strife,
These radiant ties enrich our life.

So hand in hand, we walk as one,
Through dusk and dawn, till night is done.
An endless bond, a brilliant hue,
Luminescent ties for me and you.

Forever bright, our spirits soar,
In every pulse, in every roar.
These ties we weave, our hearts ignite,
Together, we embrace the light.

Painting with Starlight

With brush in hand, I swirl the skies,
In shades of hope, my spirit flies.
Each stroke a dream, each hue a wish,
A canvas born of night's sweet kiss.

The constellations dance above,
A cosmic quilt sewn with love.
I paint the moon in silver beams,
Awakening forgotten dreams.

With every twinkle, every gleam,
The universe spills soft and cream.
I capture light, I steal a glance,
In starlit hues, I weave romance.

The night unfurls, my brush does fly,
Creating worlds where spirits sigh.
In painted skies, our souls take flight,
Together, we embrace the night.

Through every stroke, a story told,
Of love unchained, of hearts so bold.
With starlight bright, together we,
Paint our own eternal spree.

The Warmth We Share

In quiet hours, a gentle glow,
The warmth we share, a steady flow.
Through whispered dreams, through softest sighs,
A bond that blooms where stillness lies.

With every laugh, a spark ignites,
A fire that dances, pure delights.
We gather close, hearts intertwined,
In every moment, love defined.

Through storms we stand, through skies of gray,
This warmth will guide us on our way.
In darkest nights, our spirits shine,
In unity, your heart with mine.

So let the world around us change,
Together, hearts will rearrange.
In every hug, in every care,
Forever strong, this warmth we share.

Through seasons shift and time's embrace,
This warmth will never be replaced.
Hand in hand, we face each day,
In love's warm light, we'll find our way.

Glow of the Undying

In shadows deep, they softly gleam,
Unfading light, a timeless dream.
Whispers of hope in darkened skies,
A spark survives as the night sighs.

Their glow ignites the path ahead,
A fiery dance where none have tread.
Through storms of doubt, they firmly stand,
Guiding hearts with gentle hands.

They shine for those who seek and yearn,
A beacon bright, a flame to burn.
With every flicker, stories weave,
A legacy that we believe.

In every pulse, their warmth extends,
A light that loves and never ends.
Across the ages, they remain,
In endless cycles, joy and pain.

So cherish well the glow you find,
For in its flame, we intertwine.
Holding close to what we know,
Together, we'll unlock the glow.

Tethered by Stars

In the night sky, we find our place,
Orbits drawn by a gentle grace.
Each twinkling light, a tethered thread,
Connecting hearts where dreams are bred.

Through cosmic winds, our spirits soar,
Eclipsing doubts we can't ignore.
Together we dance in the vast unknown,
In unity, we'll find our home.

With every pulse of a distant star,
We reach for dreams, no matter how far.
Guided by light and the moon's soft glow,
In harmony, we learn and grow.

A constellation carved by fate,
We follow paths that love creates.
In every glance, a promise shines,
A bond unbroken by the designs.

So let us wander through endless night,
Tethered by stars, we chase the light.
For in this journey, we'll surely find,
The magic woven in heart and mind.

A Heart Lit Afloat

Upon the waves, where dreams set sail,
A heart that beats, a whispered tale.
With every swell, a pulse ignites,
A flame that dances in moonlit nights.

Through currents strong, it journeys far,
Guided by hope like a steadfast star.
Each breath a wave, each thought a breeze,
A heart afloat, embracing ease.

In gentle ripples, it finds its way,
Navigating tides that sway and play.
With open arms, it welcomes dawn,
A canvas fresh as the night is gone.

So let it drift through silent seas,
An echo soft, a sweet reprise.
In every heartbeat, waves will flow,
A heart lit bright, forever aglow.

For love is like an endless shore,
A rhythm felt forevermore.
With courage bold, we sail and drift,
A heart afloat, our greatest gift.

When Stars Align

In silence deep, the night unfolds,
A story whispered, softly told.
When stars align, the worlds embrace,
In cosmic dance, we find our place.

Each twinkle speaks of dreams once lost,
Moments cherished, no matter the cost.
As shadows fade and daylight breaks,
With open hearts, our spirit wakes.

The universe hums a tender song,
A melody where we belong.
Fate intertwines in celestial threads,
Binding all in the love it spreads.

Through echoes of the past, we'll roam,
In the light of stars, we find our home.
With every heartbeat, fate draws nigh,
When stars align, we cannot deny.

So let us cherish this cosmic chance,
In every glance, a fervent dance.
For when stars align, hearts redefined,
The magic blooms, and love is blind.

Eclipsed Affections

In twilight's grasp, we whisper low,
Hearts entwined, yet shadows grow.
A time when love feels bittersweet,
As echoes fade beneath our feet.

Silent moments hold our gaze,
Lost in a melancholic haze.
Passions dimmed by doubts we face,
Eclipsed by time, we find our place.

The moonlight dances on our skin,
Reminding us where we've been.
Yet in the dark, a flicker glows,
Through fading light, affection flows.

With every breath, we hold so tight,
Fleeting warmth in the night.
And though the stars may seem so far,
In silence, love is who we are.

Radiant Solitude

In the stillness, I find my way,
Where whispers of the heart can play.
A single light in shadows cast,
In solitude, my soul amassed.

Each thought a shimmering star afloat,
In the quiet, I stay remote.
A gentle breeze, it touches skin,
In radiant peace, I breathe within.

Through open fields, my spirit roams,
Finding solace in nature's homes.
In every rustle, every sound,
I feel the warmth of love profound.

Moments linger, gently pause,
In silence, I reflect and cause.
To cherish what the heart can know,
In radiant solitude, I grow.

Threads of Luminescence

In twilight's weave, we thread the night,
Soft glimmers dance, in soft moonlight.
A tapestry of dreams we spin,
With threads of hope, our journey begins.

Each strand a story, brightly told,
In every heart, a spark of gold.
With every weave, connections tie,
Threads of luminescence in the sky.

Glistening tales of joy and strife,
A celebration of our life.
In colors bright, we learn and grow,
Together, weaving love's warm glow.

As dawn approaches, shadows blend,
In this fabric, love transcends.
Threads of luminescence shine so clear,
In every heart, your voice I hear.

Embraced by Dawn

As morning breaks and shadows flee,
The world awakens, wild and free.
Light spills over hills and trees,
In each breath, a gentle breeze.

The sun ascends with warm embrace,
Warming hearts in its soft grace.
A golden glow on faces rise,
Whispers of hope in painted skies.

In diamond dew on petals bright,
The promise of a new delight.
Every moment sings a song,
Embraced by dawn, where we belong.

Through misty lanes, our spirits dance,
In this beauty, we find our chance.
With every ray, our worries fade,
In dawn's soft light, love won't evade.

Shadows of Radiance

In the dusk where dreams do weave,
Softly flicker shadows leave.
Whispers dance in golden light,
Casting secrets through the night.

Gentle stars begin to glow,
Cradling worlds that pulse below.
In their embrace, a silent song,
Tells of right where all belongs.

Echoes of the day retreat,
In the twilight's warm heartbeat.
Through the dark, a vision glides,
In the shadows, light abides.

Every glimmer softly plays,
In the hush of fading days.
Hope unfurls on tender wings,
As the heart within it sings.

So we wander, hand in hand,
Through the night, where dreams do stand.
With each step, a path revealed,
In the dark, our fate is sealed.

Illuminated Whispers

In the quiet, whispers flow,
Softly sparkling like the snow.
Voices wrapped in velvet night,
Share the secrets of the light.

Fleeting moments, soft and bright,
Dance upon the edge of sight.
Every shadow holds a cure,
In the silence, hearts are pure.

Gentle glimmers, brief and sweet,
Turn the dark to something neat.
Words like starlight, tender tease,
Fill our souls with gentle ease.

Fading echoes turn to dreams,
Carried forth on silver beams.
Through the shadows, we have grown,
In their depths, we've found our home.

So let the whispers light the way,
Guiding spirits come what may.
In their glow, we seek the true,
Silent truths that shine anew.

The Glow Within

Deep inside, a fire burns,
In the silence, life returns.
Through the dark, embers gleam,
Crafting pathways through the dream.

Awakened hearts begin to rise,
Drawing strength from tender skies.
In our souls, a radiant spark,
Chasing away the endless dark.

With each breath, a pulse of light,
Guiding us toward the bright.
Boundless love ignites the night,
Filling shadows with delight.

As we journey hand in hand,
Radiance in every strand.
Through the struggles, we will find,
The glow within, forever kind.

So let us shine, let spirits soar,
Finding beauty evermore.
In the stillness, truths unfold,
In our hearts, the warmth of gold.

Threads of Luminescence

In the weave of night and day,
Threads of light begin to play.
Stitched together, soft and fine,
Creating patterns truly divine.

Each connection, bright and bold,
Tells a story to behold.
Through the fabric, dreams entwine,
In their shimmer, hearts align.

Follow paths where colors blend,
In the bright, our souls transcend.
Every ray a whisper's kiss,
Binding us in timeless bliss.

In the tapestry we weave,
Hope emerges, we believe.
Through the shadows, threads will glow,
Lighting all that we can know.

Let us gather, hand in hand,
Crafting futures, bright and grand.
With each strand, our spirits sing,
In the light, we find our wings.

Secrets of the Starry Veil

Whispers of night in the silence of space,
Promises linger in the soft, dim embrace.
Stars tell of stories, of wishes and dreams,
Hidden in shadows, or so it seems.

Glimmers of hope scattered far and wide,
Floating like secrets on a gentle tide.
The cosmos holds mysteries, tight as a fist,
Yet beckons the heart with a silvery mist.

In the vastness, a dance of the light,
Revealing the paths of the brave and the bright.
Each twinkle a memory, a moment in time,
Drawing us closer with rhythm and rhyme.

Under the veil where the ancients reside,
We look to the heavens, and there we confide.
The night is alive with the tales left unsaid,
In a tapestry woven of silver and thread.

Let's gather the stars, catch the wishes that fall,
Embrace the unknown, feel the cosmic call.
For the secrets we seek are out there, unplanned,
In the heart of the universe, hand in hand.

Flickering Connections

In the midst of the chaos, a spark finds its way,
Flashing like fireflies that dance and sway.
With heartbeats entwined in a rhythm divine,
A flicker of hope and a rare, sacred sign.

Where words often falter, a glance can ignite,
A bond that transcends, shimmering light.
Bridges of laughter built on shared dreams,
Uniting our spirits with luminous beams.

Moments of silence where solace is found,
Flickers of joy in the world all around.
An echo of love that forever will stay,
Binding our hearts in an intricate way.

Through trials and sorrows, we stand side by side,
With flickering candles our hearts open wide.
Like stars that keep shining through dark velvet skies,
In the depths of our souls, the connection never dies.

So cherish the flickers, the moments we share,
In the tapestry woven with tenderest care.
For love is the light, an eternal reflection,
A spark in the shadows, our flickering connection.

A Glance Through Gilded Rifts

Through the golden rifts, a glimpse of the past,
Moments of laughter forever cast.
Time weaves its magic with delicate grace,
A glance through the rifts, where memories trace.

In echoes of laughter, the heart starts to sing,
With each gilded moment, sweet memories cling.
The sun and the shadows, a dance on the floor,
Carving out stories, forevermore.

Wonders unraveled in the light's gentle glow,
Like wisps of the wind, where soft breezes blow.
We gather the fragments, all that we find,
A treasure of time in the fabric entwined.

As we peer through the rifts, with wonder and awe,
Life's vivid tapestry, fragile yet raw.
In moments of beauty, our spirits take flight,
A glance through the gilded, igniting the night.

So cherish the visions, let them unfold,
In whispers of stories, in dust made of gold.
For within gilded rifts, our past shines so bright,
Guiding our hearts with the warmth of their light.

When Shadows Dance

When shadows dance beneath the pale moonlight,
They weave through the trees, taking flight.
In the stillness of night, their secrets are spun,
In whispers and sighs, until the night's done.

They play on the edges, with grace and finesse,
A ballet of darkness, a delicate mess.
Drifting like whispers in a soft, gentle breeze,
Enticing the heart, putting the mind at ease.

Each flicker of movement, a tale to be told,
In the quiet of night, where magic unfolds.
In shadows' embrace, there's comfort and peace,
A space where our worries can momentarily cease.

Through the veil of the dark, let imagination soar,
Where shadows bring visions that we can't ignore.
For in the dance of the night, we often find grace,
An invitation to dream in a shadowy place.

So let the shadows lead you, take you away,
To a realm where the heart can freely play.
In the whispers of night, let your spirit enhance,
And lose yourself softly when shadows dance.

Veil of Glimmer

In twilight's grace, the stars awake,
Whispers of night, in shadows break.
The moon's soft glow, a tender guide,
As dreams and truth begin to glide.

Beneath the veil, secrets reside,
Glimmers of hope, that hearts confide.
With each breath, the magic swells,
In every heart, a story dwells.

Night's gentle hand, it cradles all,
In silence deep, the echoes call.
Every flicker, a tale to weave,
In the glimmer, the soul believes.

Through starry paths, we find our way,
In midnight's hush, where shadows play.
The veil of glimmer, a sacred space,
Where light and dark, in harmony, trace.

Eternal dance, the cosmos spins,
In the quiet, a universe grins.
Veil of glimmer, forever bright,
Guiding us home, through the night.

The Art of Illumination

In strokes of gold, the canvas flows,
Each hue a whisper, as daylight glows.
With brush in hand, the heart will sing,
Painting dreams, the light will bring.

Through shadowed realms, we find our spark,
In every corner, we leave a mark.
The art of life, in colors bright,
Illuminates the darkest night.

Each stroke a step, each shade a tale,
In every moment, we shall not fail.
With passion fierce, the canvas breathes,
The art of love, in every piece.

In twilight's glow, the images dance,
A wondrous world, awash in chance.
Through vibrant hues, our spirits soar,
The art of illumination, forever more.

With every ray, our stories blend,
Creating beauty, with no end.
The brush of life, in hand we trust,
Transforming moments, from dust to dust.

Resplendent Moments

In fleeting time, we find our grace,
Each second a jewel, in life's embrace.
With laughter bright, we paint the air,
Resplendent moments, beyond compare.

Through simple joys, our hearts take flight,
A dance of shadows, bathed in light.
In whispered dreams, we find our home,
In every heartbeat, love's gentle poem.

From dawn's first blush to evening's sigh,
Time weaves stories, as moments fly.
In nature's arms, we pause, and feel,
The beauty in life, so pure, so real.

Each glance exchanged beneath the sun,
A symphony, in harmony spun.
Resplendent moments, we treasure dear,
In every heartbeat, love is near.

As stars align, we raise our gaze,
To cherish life, in wondrous ways.
Each moment glows, a memory bright,
Resplendent moments, our guiding light.

Glowing Threads of Fate

In life's grand loom, the threads entwine,
Every twist and turn, a sign divine.
With gentle hands, we weave and spin,
Glowing threads of fate, beneath our skin.

Through trials faced, we gather strength,
In every heartbeat, we find our length.
Connections forged, in passion's fire,
The fabric of dreams, we never tire.

With each encounter, a stitch is made,
In laughter shared, no joy shall fade.
The threads of fate, a tapestry wide,
In colors bold, our hearts collide.

In times of darkness, the glow will shine,
A guiding light, through every line.
The web of life, a dance so grand,
Glowing threads of fate, in love we stand.

As journeys cross, and stories blend,
In every moment, we shall transcend.
With glowing threads, our lives embrace,
We weave our destiny, in time and space.

Shining Bonds

In the quiet light, we stand,
Hearts entwined, hand in hand.
Through storms and sunny days,
Our friendship forever stays.

Each laugh and tear we share,
A treasure beyond compare.
With every shared embrace,
We find our special place.

Together we rise and fall,
Answering each other's call.
In every glance, we see,
The strength of you and me.

Though time may fade and fly,
These bonds shall never die.
In the light of trust, we soar,
Forever friends, forever more.

Glow and Grow

In the dawn, our dreams ignite,
Nurtured by the morning light.
With every step we take,
We find the joys we make.

Hope is planted like a seed,
Watered with our every need.
Through trials, through delight,
We bloom, we shine so bright.

With every lesson learned,
A new page has been turned.
In the garden of our days,
We flourish in many ways.

Together, hand in hand,
Creating something grand.
As we blossom, hearts unite,
In a glow that feels so right.

In the Embrace of Radiance

In the warmth of your embrace,
I find my heart's true place.
Bathed in golden light,
Everything feels just right.

With every whispered word,
Feelings deeply stirred.
In the silence, we connect,
A bond we can protect.

Stars above us gently shine,
A cosmic love divine.
Each moment, bright and clear,
I cherish having you near.

Through the shadows, we will glide,
With you always by my side.
In the glow of every night,
We find our purest light.

The Light That Weaves Us

In moments shared, we weave a thread,
A tapestry of words unsaid.
With every laugh, every tear,
The light brings us ever near.

Through shadows and through dreams,
Life is not all that it seems.
With purpose, we shall find
The brilliance intertwined.

Regardless of the paths we take,
A bond that will not break.
In unity, we stand tall,
Answering each other's call.

As the dawn breaks new and bright,
We radiate our light.
Together in life's embrace,
We shine with love's pure grace.